Mary Baron

LETTERS
FOR THE
NEW ENGLAND DEAD

David R. Godine

FOR *This lady . . . my child, Cordelia*

David R. Godine Publisher
Boston, Massachusetts

LCC 73-84885
ISBN 0-87923-083-5

'With time I've learned . . .' and 'Lines for a Critic' first appeared in *Folio*. 'Cordelia,' 'For an Angry Poet,' 'Personal Epitaph,' 'You ask an exercise . . . ,' and 'Landscape: American Northwest' first appeared in the *Southern Review*. 'With My Child,' 'Ninth Month' (an earlier version), sections 1 and 2 of the 'Letters for the New England Dead,' and 'For an Egyptian Boy' first appeared in *Back Door*. 'Anniversary Evening,' 'November Milkweed,' 'Last Summer We Moved,' and 'Elegy for an Old Lady' first appeared in *Counter/Measures*. 'Love Letter' and 'Pythia' appeared in the *Maryland Poetry Review*. The present version of 'Ninth Month' appeared in *Weeds*.

Designed by Carol Shloss

Number 4 in the
FIRST GODINE POETRY
CHAPBOOK SERIES

Jan Schreiber, General Editor

Letters

for the

New England Dead

For an Egyptian Boy, died c. 700 B.C.

The Kelsey Museum, Ann Arbor

It is a hollow child, delicate, frail,
A beautiful thin husk, a leather case
To keep the spirit in.
                    'The body is
A Temple of the Holy Ghost.' I told
The nuns this was impossible; I see,
Here, how it's done. Shrunk down, hardened, refined,
The flesh distills into a beetle's shell,
Sacred despite disgust, protective, real.

Last Summer We Moved

Flat land, no hills or trees encompassing,
And me, driving. Once I got into
The township dump, just looking for
A quiet road, that went on without cars.
Once I got out, to lie down in a road
Between two farms, crying because the sky
Had come too low, pressing against my back
In the hot emptiness between the wheat.
Driving, cursing the traffic signs MUST TURN
Toward what? no trees, no shade, no people in the place
And blankness coming, like that sky, in dreams.
Automatic months – lived out, survived,
They haunt me like childbirth. I turn to them
With the exhausted smile a mother has,
Greeting her infant, thinking of the pain.

Ninth Month

I feel the child within me slowly move,
Turning in the dark water, sensing the rush
Of heavy fluid out – out through the bones
To air.
      Small one, I know your helplessness
And haste. Wanting poems, I turn in this dark
Winter, watching for light, waiting for words
And you.
      I mumbled curses, giving birth,
Pushing the child to come, wanting her out
Ready or not. Love, like the poem, comes later.

With My Child at the Museum of Natural History

Her favorite is the Mastodon, a thing
So gray and blundering even his bones
Look awkward. He reminds her of our dog.
But I prefer a smaller scale, and choose
Least Weasel from a case on Third Floor East.
I like him for the humor of his name
And for the delicate alertness of
The stance in which he died. My daughter says
He's little, like a doll, and finds him dull.
We both reach out for what we recognize
Among the deadened wonders of this place.
My mother always said she liked a wake.

8

Pythia

In rain on Friday afternoon, at dusk,
The squirrels in our yard are sorting out
Remnants of autumn; useful, edible
Damp bits of dying vegetation. I
Have no such hoards. I am in winter calm
And silence. Here among my books, I sit;
I do not read. Outside, my daughter stirs,
A quiet accusation. Minutes pass.
I sit in service of a voiceless god.

Cordelia

The depths of solitude that she can reach
On any cool, green morning, as she swings
In long slow rhythms through the backyard peace.
I watch her waken daily in its sway,
Lulling herself from sleep, until she sings
Plain nonsense as her greeting to the day.

If, rarely, I can touch that central quiet,
I find it by old music; fine, fierce words
And in the dark. I've never seen the light
Even of winter evenings on such calm
As that my child's morning rite affords.
I only watch; nor can I match her song.

Aubade for a Daughter

You sleep stretched out between us, forgetful
Of nights you drowsed, curled like your tiny fists,
A pink half-moon, as safe as porcupines.
Tonight you were a thin, sharp-angled X.
Your bones have taken over; you are hinged.
Oh my fat sweet grub, you are unrolled.
Inside your skin you're an arrow. – Small fern,
Straightening quietly within our shade.

Elegy for an Old Lady

It was your harshness that I most admired,
Abrasive yankee cunning, used as love.
Taming the Irish boys your daughters wed,
Spinning them on your voice, you talked until
They reached a Puritan gentility.
Always a lady, always correct and fierce,
You drove us through our lives, rocking, rocking,
Pushing against that chair, pushing us on.
I can't imagine peace you would accept.
Sure of salvation, you prepared for it
As if for war. Oh your aggressive God
Will have a task for you, Frances. Praising,
Praising, perhaps; keeping angels in line.

Meditation in the Public Gardens

I have learned how to hold the mind down close.
Invariant and dogged, on the move,
It ponders out my days, proceeding like
Those silver-haired old ladies in blue hats
Who march in stubborn, disapproving pride
Through public parks where once they walked as girls.
Both they and I are circumscribed. We go
With narrowed vision down straight patterned paths,
Not by our choice. The ladies by their age
And sanctified tradition cannot step
Onto the grass, or note that others do.
And only madness would unleash this mind.

For an Angry Poet, Who Requested a Poem on War

To end the conversation, as attack,
You ask me can I sanction murderers,
And write in form within a formless world?
Well yes, I can do both. I've known the urge,
Half human, speak of death that's not my own,
And I have listened. That's the sin itself,
As close, at least, as you can get to it
Without the doing. In the old church law
The one counts as the other, as it should.
Guilt constitutes a sanction, I should think.
As to the form: A fence can keep things out,
I've found, as well as keeping in, and I
Have more to keep away than I suspect
You've met or even dreamt of yet. If then
It should get into words somehow, something
You'd never meant to say, you've the excuse,
To soothe your pride, that it was led in by
The form or by the rhyme or some such thing.
This helps more than a little, more than you'd guess.
Pride should be closely guarded, it will help
When nothing else is any help at all.

Now to the poem on war. You'll not be pleased,
I know, with what it is I say in it.
It's not a poem of war as you would know
The word. It's as I know it, private, hard,
And not a social act. What you don't see,
And what I do, is that they're both the same.

14

You'd bring the war down to one bleeding child
While I would start right here at home with me
And not make all that journey into Asia.

But you want speech of war, the larger kind,
Then I'll refer to one I've felt and know,
The old one that our fathers held, it's not
This closer one you've chosen as your cause.
I have here in the house, here in the room,
A Nazi general's flag, but not stretched on
The wall, defiance of the present case,
A gesture of the general discontent,
Not that at all. It has a special place,
Is carefully and honorably kept
As a tradition. We have still a few
Old honored remnants, on my father's side,
About the house and this is one of them.
My father won it in the war, but not
By arms. And here, perhaps, I should explain:
Bad timing and the fortunes of the war
Arranged it so that we should never meet,
Father and daughter, but I know of him,
Beyond the name and dates, that he was skilled
In building things and that, throughout the war,
They called him Kelly, egged him on to wear
The green in place of his white sailor's scarf.
I'd do a thing like that, given the pride
Of race, which I'm afraid is lost by now.

And it's because I recognize the fear
And damn fool pride that lie behind the thing,
Foolish as it is (I know it cost
Him quite a bit of harrassment, his chief
Not being Irish), that I feel I sense
The man and, even without meeting, feel
I comprehend just what it was he meant
In sending home that flag as his last gift.
He said he got it from an officer,
A nameless prisoner of war, in France.
A man my father had dragged after him
For quite some time, there being then no camp
Which they could reach. They never spoke. Simply,
They could not. There was not a word that both
Could understand. But they had grown in time
Quite used to one another, and one night,
My father very ill with what it was
That killed him in the end, they were two men
In mud and not a war. One gave his flag
As blanket to the other one and came,
My father said, cautiously, in fear
The gift would be refused. That it was not
Does not so much surprise me. Men in time
Of horror rise into humanity
With what would seem to be surprising ease.
What, when I came to understand it, held
My admiration, made me look again
At what it was I had inherited

16

From people whom I hardly knew, was what
His parents rose to when they kept the flag.
They kept the thing they hated, only asked,
When I was grown, if I could tell them what
He'd meant by it. I think, you know, from what
I know of him, that he meant nothing much
But just what you'd expect. That sometimes men
Are reasonable creatures, even kind,
And when they are that we should know of it.
And then, perhaps, this too, since he did ask
That it be kept with his own casket flag.
That men can shelter under anything,
And still be men, if we will only notice.

Alternate Reading:
On a Sequence of Short Poems

Read in controlled sequence
These are defense.
The mind held here is old,
Sufficient, cold.
But each, read separately,
Can frighten me.
More than the mind is there.
I also hear,
Not by the poet's choice,
An aged voice.

You ask an exercise in the exact,
A poem, also record of the fact.
There's this involved: some years of love, no speech,
No touch and no forgetfulness. The reach
Of mind exhausted now, I fear an end,
By my own hand, perhaps, and soon. I send
You this in answer, though I know in part
It's not a poem. Terror is not art.

This silence in the mind, I know, can lead
Me down to madness. I have been there once
And will not go again. I know: first, thought
Is stilled and in the quiet one can find
No single word within. There is the fear
The thing will stop, and then it finally does,
And all the self goes huddled with the pain.
It must be what the transmigration of
A soul is like, pain and uncertainty,
Coming and going, with a little while
To live as people do who do not know
Of this. I will not go again. Instead,
I'd close the cycle off myself, and sleep
However long it is decreed we should.

Ite, missa est

He would not take me back. He'd know I came
Home only as a tired child, to rest.
Introibo ad altare Dei, I'd come
But only go again, and in between
I'd hide myself in His oblivion,
Hoarding all my strength for human tasks.
No, I cannot go home there, anymore.
But still, within this plainsong's Latin peace,
I say 'My Jesus, mercy' to the dark.

With time, I've learned to take my coffee black.
A small and strange accomplishment, you think?
Well, more's involved than leaving out the milk.
Cliff Klingenhagen knew. He chose his drink.

November Milkweed

Swollen and green, obscene with leaking sap,
Last week they made no noise when the wind blew.
Today I hear them rustle in a breeze;
They're drying out. Pods stiffen on the stalks,
Holding their empty wombs to the cold sun.
All day, I hear them harden into death.

T.V. Special: The Rockies, 1846

Bald Tooth and *Bitter Root*, down in between
A mining town crowded against the creek.
Here, caught within the black and washed out gray
Of a daguerrotype, the tall men stare.
Under their hats they have the look of kin.
This is communal madness, wholesale lust
For unresponsive metal, bitter root.

Landscape: American Northwest

This earth gives in too easy, comes up green
Without the aid of ancestry, the pride,
We need for battle with New England's rock.
There are no monuments in stone, our walls,
The proof of labor and the land subdued.
Even the tombstones here rest by the road,
Akin to earth, not stark and vigilant
And halfway up some hill that points ascent.
These dead have all lain down and found their peace
In woods which could not shelter our hard souls,
In insufficient shade, without the reach
Of one dark pine, to stand for what we fear.

Letters for the New England Dead

1 ANNE BRADSTREET

Anne,
I think of you, the Massachusetts coast,
Your long Quarternions bound up in rhyme –
Hysteria, thrown out at empty fields.
The Earl of Lincoln ran a different house.
> *I found a new world at which my heart rose.*
> *I was convinced it was the Way of God;*
> *I submitted to it.*

2 EMILY DICKINSON

In Emily's Amherst, the tombstones talk.
> *This stone is meant by its color*
> *To signify the moral character ...*

Their correspondences were absolute;
Men were so small, against New England snows.
> *I was the slightest in the house –*
> *I took the smallest room.*

Lavinia pries; your mother lives too long.
Inside the beautiful old house, you bleach
Out white.

3 ANNE BRADSTREET

Anne,
I know you moved against the wilderness
Slowly, feeling the weight, the children in
Your womb. The men cut down the trees. Inside,
You hacked your way in rhymes to Lincolnshire,
To England, where the way to God was clear.

26

In this new land He comes like the gaunt skulls
Carved on the Concord tombs, beating black wings
Above your bed until the fever breaks.
Next time, you find Him in another fear.
With humble hearts and mouths put i' the dust
Let's say He's Merciful, as well as Just.
Say it in poems that sing like the Bay Psalms,
Incantatory, desperate, write out God
And pin Him down to Mercy, on the page.

4   JOHN COTTON I

When I think of the sweet and gracious company
That at Boston once I had
And of the long peace of a fruitful ministry
For twenty years enjoyed,
The joy that I had in all that happiness
Doth still so much refresh me,
That the grief to be cast out into a wilderness
Doth not so much distress me.

Liar. The grief that breaks to speech goes deep,
Dark as the sea waves that you crossed, coming,
At God's command, to godforsaken lands.
You must have wondered why He needed you
To sow His word over the empty fields.

5   EPILOGUE

The Concord dead lie cold, taut in the earth.
The winged skulls shriek: *None shall escape the wrath*
Of the King of Terrors.

27

Mary Reynolds Kelley, 1920-1966

Mother, I hope that you will reach,
And rest within, abiding peace,
Whether in that Eternal Birth
You half believed in, or in earth.

Personal Epitaph: Lines for a Tombstone

Wrapped in soft peace, on every side,
Rest those who, acquiescent, died.
I lived, and now I wake, with rage,
Who chose this death, instead of age.

Love Letter

It snows now even when the sun is out.
The day your letter came, I stayed inside –
All day. My hair is growing long. The dog
Has had her puppies; we gave them away.
Mondays I teach. Every goddamn time
I pass the place, I think of you. My dear,
What can I say to you, at such a distance?

Anniversary Evening

for Dennis

The house is under water in this light,
Drifting beneath the green of the near trees.
Inside, speechless at dusk, we slowly move
From room to room, bodies maneuvering
Against resistance of warm air. The child
Falls asleep before dark. Reading, we go
Nowhere, together, in the evening light.
Held in the bowl of years, we are like fish
Circling endlessly, calm in clear water.
Rising to go to bed, we are silent,
Relaxing against the air, against each other.

Lines for a Critic

You say I live to use my life in verse
And this appalls you. Sir, I have done worse.